THE BAH
BLUEPRINT
FROM PAYCHECK
TO PORTFOLIO

**LEARN HOW TO STRUCTURE
YOUR MONEY LIKE A BUSINESS –
PLAN, INVEST, REINVEST**

ASK ANTWAUN

BAH Blueprint

From Paycheck to Portfolio

ISBN: 979-8-9936505-3-1

Published by AskAntwaun Media

All inquiries: AskAntwaun@gmail.com
Printed in the United States of America

Book Design by Williams DocuPrep
www.williamsdocuprep.com

Table of Contents

Acknowledgements

To every Soldier, Sailor, Airman, Marine, and guardian who serves this book is for you. You've sacrificed time, comfort, and certainty in service to your country. Now it's time to serve your future.

To my family, thank you for your patience, support, and belief when I worked late nights building this vision. And to every client, colleague, and mentor who shared their stories, your experiences shaped every page.

Service doesn't stop when you hang up the uniform. Sometimes, it just changes missions.

Introduction

Money Without a Mission

Every service member knows what it means to have a mission. There's a plan, a timeline, and a clear objective. But when it comes to money, most don't have one. For years, I treated money like it was just fuel: something to get me from one paycheck to the next. My BAH, COLA, and basic pay were just numbers in, bills out. I didn't realize I was running my finances without a mission plan, and that's exactly how most people stay stuck in the same financial loop year after year.

Think about it. The military runs on structured schedules, SOPs, accountability. But our personal finances? Usually chaos. We spend, we save a little, and we hope things "work out. Hope is not a strategy.

This book is about changing that, about transforming your finances from reactive to intentional. Because the truth is, you don't need to make more money to build wealth. You just need to assign every dollar a job.

The BAH Blueprint gives you the framework to turn your pay into profit, not by cutting out every coffee or living like a monk, but by structuring your money like a business. Every paycheck becomes an investment in your future, every expense a calculated decision, and every benefit (especially your BAH) a tool for growth.

Inside, we'll cover:

- How to design a simple, automated budgeting system that works even when life gets hectic.

- How to eliminate debt strategically, not emotionally.

- How to use your BAH to buy appreciating assets instead of paying someone else's mortgage.

- How to think like an investor, even if you've never owned a stock or property before.

This is not about perfection. It's about control. It's about building a repeatable process for wealth, one that works whether you're stationed overseas, stateside, or starting over. Money without a mission gets spent. Money with a blueprint builds freedom.

Chapter 1

From Paycheck to Purpose – The Military Mindset Shift

In the military, every mission starts with a plan. You wouldn't move without an objective, a route, or a backup plan. But when it comes to money? Most of us are just winging it.

We check our LES, see what hit the account, and start spending. Rent, car, food, maybe a splurge or two, then it's back to waiting for the 1st and 15th. That's not a strategy. That's survival.

The Disconnect

Here's the thing: You already have the mindset needed to master money. The problem isn't discipline; it's direction. The military teaches accountability, structure, and execution. But it rarely teaches how to use those same skills on your personal finances.

Think about it: You plan your missions, your PT schedule, and your gear layout all with precision. So why not your paycheck? Your money needs a mission too.

Money Follows Orders

Every dollar in your bank account is a soldier under your command. If you don't give it an order, it'll go AWOL.

Some will get lost in impulse buys, others in subscriptions you forgot about. But if you tell every dollar what its job is—save, invest, grow—suddenly you're in control of the battlefield. And that's what separates financial chaos from financial freedom.

Reframing the Mission

You've probably heard, "I just need to make more money." But that's like saying, "I need more soldiers," when what you really need is a better strategy. Wealth isn't built by how much you make; it's built by how effectively you deploy what you have. Your job is to shift from *earning money* to *commanding money*.

Here's the mindset framework:

- **Discipline = Direction.** You already have it. Now apply it.

- **Structure = Freedom.** A plan gives you control, not restriction.

- **Repetition = Wealth.** Consistency beats big moves every time.

Your New Mission: Purpose Over Paycheck

From this point forward, your pay isn't just income; it's capital. Capital for your family's future, your next PCS opportunity, your first rental property, your investments, and your legacy.

The moment you stop viewing your paycheck as spending money and start treating it like mission fuel, everything changes. You don't need to make six figures. You just need a six-step plan and that's what this blueprint gives you.

Chapter 2

Building Your Financial Formation – The Budget System

Every successful mission starts with organization. You don't deploy without formation. You don't train without structure. You don't move without knowing who's responsible for what. Money works the same way.

A budget isn't a restriction; it's formation. It's how you align every dollar under your command and make sure none of them wander off. And once you start treating your money like your unit, you'll see something powerful happening, clarity replaces chaos.

The Purpose of the Budget

Let's make this clear. A budget isn't about saying

no to things you want. It's about saying *yes* with confidence to the things that matter.

You already have the discipline. You wake up early, show up on time, and follow through. The same structure that keeps your career on track can keep your money moving in the right direction.

1. A strong budget gives you three things:

2. Control – You decide where your money goes, not the other way around.

3. Clarity – You can see exactly what's working and what's wasteful.

4. Confidence – You can plan for what's next instead of hoping for the best.

The Four-Account System

Most people overcomplicate budgeting. You don't need fancy spreadsheets or twelve accounts. You need formation: four accounts, each with a clear mission.

Here's the breakdown:

1. Operations Account (Primary Checking)

Mission: Handle your bills, necessities, and recurring payments.

Example: Rent/mortgage, utilities, insurance, car payment.

Think of this as HQ, where the action happens, but not where soldiers hang out for long.

2. Reserve Account (Savings)

Mission: Emergency fund and short-term goals (PCS costs, travel, etc.)

Start with one month of expenses, build up to six. This is your financial "ready reserve." You don't touch it unless ordered.

3. Investment Account (Growth)

Mission: Build wealth.

This is where your TSP, Roth IRA, or brokerage account contributions come from. You don't spend this money; it works behind the scenes.

4. Freedom Account (Fun Money)

Mission: Maintain morale.

A small, guilt-free spending fund for entertainment, hobbies, or date nights. Every mission has downtime; this keeps the plan sustainable.

The 70/20/10 Framework

Now that your accounts are in formation, here's how to allocate your income:

- **70% – Needs and Essentials**

  This covers everything in your Operations Account. (Rent, food, insurance, gas, bills.)

- **20% – Future Growth**

  This includes savings and investments. Split it 10% to your Reserve Account and 10% to your Investment Account.

- **10% – Lifestyle & Giving**

  Your Freedom Account and generosity bucket. Whether that's donations, travel, or self-care, this keeps your mission human.

Adjust the percentages as your rank and responsibilities grow. The point is consistency, giving every dollar direction.

Automation: Your Secret Weapon

You know the beauty of a military schedule? It runs whether you're tired or not. That's how your budget should work.

Automate as much as possible:

- Automatic transfers to savings and investments.

- Automatic bill pay for recurring expenses.

- Separate debit card for "Freedom" spending.

Automation removes emotion from the equation: no guilt, no guessing, just execution.

A Budget Isn't Static; It Evolves

Every PCS, promotion, or family change is a new mission. Your formation shifts with it. Don't treat your budget like a contract; treat it like a strategy. Adjust, refine, and move forward.

When you start operating this way, your money stops slipping through your fingers. It starts working in formation toward your goals, your wealth, and your freedom.

Chapter 3

The Debt War – Eliminating Liabilities Strategically

In the military, no one wins a war without identifying the enemy. In personal finance, that enemy is debt. Debt is like a silent ambush. You don't feel the attack right away but every month, it chips away at your freedom. It's not just about the money you owe; it's about the control you lose when someone else decides what you owe and when you owe it. If you want to build wealth, you have to win the debt war first.

Step One: Know the Battlefield

Most people hate looking at their debt. But hiding from it doesn't make it disappear, it just gives it time to multiply. So the first step is recon. You can't win a battle without knowing your targets.

Write down every debt you have:

- Credit cards
- Car loans
- Personal loans
- Student loans
- Payday loans (if any, they're the most danger-ous enemy in the field)

For each, note:

- Total balance
- Minimum payment
- Interest rate
- Due date

Now, rank them. You've just mapped your battle-field.

Step Two: Choose Your Strategy

There are two proven debt-elimination strategies: the *Snowball* and the *Avalanche*. Both work, but they serve different tactical goals.

1. The Snowball Method – Momentum First.

You pay off your smallest debts first, regardless of

interest rate. Every time you eliminate one, you build confidence and speed.

Example:

If you have:

- $500 credit card
- $2,000 car repair loan
- $4,000 personal loan

Start with the $500 one. Once it's gone, roll that payment into the next one. This is about *psychological victory*. Small wins build big momentum.

2. The Avalanche Method – Efficiency First.

You target the highest-interest debt first. This saves you more money long-term, but can feel slower at the start.

Example:

If your $4,000 personal loan is at 15% and your $500 card is at 8%, you start with the $4,000. This method is for those who like optimization over motivation. Either one works what matters is commitment and consistency. Pick your weapon and execute.

Step Three: Eliminate and Reassign

Once a debt is paid off, don't relax reassign the funds. If you were paying $200/month on a loan, that $200 now becomes your next debt payment, savings boost, or investment fund.

In the Army, we call that force multiplication — taking freed-up resources and redirecting them toward the next objective. This is how you turn debt freedom into financial acceleration.

Step Four: Understand Good vs. Bad Debt

Not all debt is the enemy some can be a strategic ally.

Good Debt:

- Helps you acquire appreciating assets (real estate, education, business investments).

- Has manageable interest and clear ROI.

Bad Debt:

- Funds lifestyle wants (cars, clothes, unnecessary upgrades).

- Offers no financial return.

- Costs more than it earns.

The rule is simple: if it doesn't make you money, it's a liability. Good debt is like a skilled contractor: temporary, useful, and pays for itself. Bad debt is a lazy roommate, always around, never helping.

Step Five: Protect Your Progress

As you eliminate debt, new opportunities will show up higher credit limits, new offers, "easy financing." Don't fall for it. That's like winning a firefight and running back into the open field.

Stay protected:

- Keep your credit cards open for history, but use them lightly and pay in full.

- Set auto-reminders or autopay for every loan.

- Don't co-sign for anyone. Ever.

Each of these steps fortifies your financial defense system.

Victory Looks Like Freedom

The day you pay off your final debt, something shifts. You stop working for your past and start building your future. It's not just about having zero balance it's about having zero stress.

That's when you're ready for the next phase: turning the cash you were using to fight debt into capital that works for you.

Chapter 4

BAH as a Business Asset – Turning Housing Allowance into Equity

If you're in the military, you already receive one of the most powerful, misunderstood wealth tools in existence: **BAH — Basic Allowance for Housing.**

It's guaranteed, tax-free, and consistent. Yet most service members treat it like rent money instead of investment fuel.

Let's change that.

The Misunderstanding

When I first joined the Army, I thought BAH was a housing stipend, free money to make life a little easier. It covered my rent, my utilities, and sometimes even a little extra.

But what I didn't realize was this: BAH isn't meant to make you comfortable; it's meant to make you capable. That money is an investment tool. It's your built-in leverage for creating long-term equity, ownership, and cash flow.

The only question is: Whose pocket does your BAH build wealth for? Yours or your landlord's?

The Real Math

Let's take a practical example.

Say you're an E-6 with dependents stationed in Hawaii, receiving $3,200 per month in BAH. If you rent for a 3-year tour, that's $3,200 × 36 months = $115,200 Gone. Zero return.

But if you buy even a modest townhome, you start redirecting that same allowance into ownership.

Let's say:

- Purchase price: $500,000

- Loan: VA loan at 5.5%

- Monthly payment: ≈ $3,200 (covered entirely by BAH)

After 3 years, here's what happens:

- You've paid down roughly $27,000 in principal

- Assuming your home appreciates 3% annually → value increases by $46,000+

- That's over $70,000 in built equity, using the same BAH that would've vanished as rent.

That's the difference between spending money and deploying money.

Your BAH Is a Business Budget

Start thinking of your BAH as business capital. Every month, Uncle Sam gives you tax-free funding for your housing. How you use it determines whether it becomes a cost (rent) or an asset (ownership). Your goal isn't just to find a place to live; it's to position your BAH to work.

That could mean:

- Buying a home you'll later rent out when you PCS.

- Using a house-hack strategy (renting out a room or unit).

- Partnering with your spouse to acquire a duplex instead of a single-family.

- Buying in high-demand rental markets to pre-serve resale and rental flexibility.

When you start structuring BAH decisions like business investments, you'll realize you're already funded to start your portfolio.

Golden Nugget Tip: The 3-3 Rule

If you're buying while in service, keep this in mind:

- **3 Years Minimum Hold:** Aim to own each property for at least 3 years, long enough to build equity, ride appreciation, and offset transaction costs.

- **3% Appreciation Goal:** Even modest markets usually deliver this annually. Anything more is a bonus.

This rule helps you stay grounded and strategic instead of impulsive.

Common Objections (and the Truth)

- **"I don't want to deal with being a landlord."**

  → Property managers exist for a reason. You can automate nearly everything.

- **"What if I PCS somewhere I can't afford to buy?"**

→ That's fine. The key is owning *somewhere*. You can buy in a previous duty station, your home of record, or an investor-friendly market.

- **"What if the market crashes?"**

    → It could. But even then, if your tenants (or your BAH) cover the payment, your investment survives until the market recovers. Time beats timing.

Equity: The Silent Pay Raise

Something most military families never calculate is every time you pay your mortgage, your net worth quietly increases. That's equity, the part of your home you actually own.

You can't build equity renting, but you can by owning. And equity opens doors to the next phase: leveraging what you've built.

Chapter 5

Investing 101: Making Your Money Earn Rank

Most service members think investing is "for later," after retirement, after promotion, after the kids are older. The problem with that thinking is simple: money only grows with time and consistency. If you wait until everything is perfect, you miss the years that do the heavy lifting.

This chapter isn't about day trading, memes, or guessing the market. It's about building a simple, military-style investing system that works while you're deployed, on TDY, or PCSing. You don't need to be a financial advisor. You need a plan, a rank structure, and automation.

Why You Need to Invest Even If You're Buying Real Estate

A lot of military investors go straight to real estate, and that's good. You should own doors. But real wealth is **layered**, not **either-or**.

- Real estate = cash flow + appreciation + tax benefits.

- Investing (stocks/ETFs) = liquidity + diversification + compound growth.

If all your wealth is in property and something happens like a vacancy, a big repair, or a PCS at the wrong time, you don't want to be stuck. Your investment accounts are the quiet soldiers in the background, growing whether you're working or not.

The Military Risk Lens: Logistics vs. Special Ops

Let's make this plain.

- **Low Risk = Logistics.** Slow, reliable, mission critical. Not flashy, but always moving.

- **Medium Risk = Infantry.** Balanced, flexible, still disciplined.

- **High Risk = Special Ops.** Big upside, but only for specific missions, and you don't send the whole unit.

Your money should be deployed the same way.

Tier 1: Logistics Money (Low Risk)

This is your backbone. You don't gamble this.

What goes here:

- TSP in an index-heavy mix (C, S, I or Lifecycle if you want set-and-forget).

- Broad market index funds (like an S&P 500 index fund).

- High-yield savings for short-term goals.

Why: These grow steadily over time. Not exciting, but that's not their job. Their job is to always be moving forward.

Set this on autopilot:

- Allotment from LES straight to TSP.

- Monthly automatic transfer to investment account.

- "Pay yourself first" before bills, before Amazon.

Tier 2: Infantry Money (Medium Risk)

This is for building faster.

What goes here:

- Sector ETFs (tech, healthcare, defense).

- Dividend ETFs.

- Target-date funds outside of TSP.

Why: Still diversified, but a little more aggressive. You're saying, "I want more growth than savings, but I'm not trying to blow the whole bag."

This is a good zone for dual-military couples or E-5/E-6 with stable BAH who want to grow but have kids, cars, and life to think about.

Tier 3: Special Ops Money (High Risk)

This is not where you start. This is where you graduate.

What goes here:

- Individual stocks

- Small-cap/high-volatility ETFs

- Short-term plays you actually researched

Rules for this tier:

1. Never more than 10–15% of your investing to-tal.

2. Don't use emergency money.

3. Don't use BAH you need for rent/mortgage.

4. If you can't explain the investment in two sentences, don't buy it.

High risk should never be fueled by boredom.

Index Funds vs. ETFs vs. Individual Stocks (Plain English)

- **Index fund:** "Give me the whole market." Easy, low cost. Good for beginners.

- **ETF:** Same idea as an index fund, but trades like a stock. Good for flexibility.

- **Individual stock:** "I believe in *this* company." Higher upside, higher risk.

- **Mutual fund:** Managed for you, but usually higher fees.

For 90% of people, 90% of the time, the answer is: broad index fund + automatic investing.

Automation: Your Financial Battle Rhythm

If you have to remember to invest, you won't.

Here's the simple flow:

1. LES hits.

2. Automatic transfer $\rightarrow$ Roth IRA / brokerage (set amount).

3. Pre-selected investments buy automatically.

4. Review once a month, not every day.

This is how you win while deployed, while in school, while PCSing, while life is messy.

How Much Should I Invest?

Use the 10 / 15 / 20 Rule:

- 10% if you're just starting / tight budget.

- 15% if you're stable.

- 20%+ if you're dual military or housing is covered/base housing.

And remember BAH can fund investing if your mortgage is lower than your BAH. That's the whole strategy of this series.

What If I Start Late?

Start anyway. You're not behind; you just have to be more intentional.

- Automate a higher amount.

- Add lump sums (tax refunds, COLA, bonus, incentive pays).

- Cut dead expenses and convert to investing.

Wealth is about discipline, not age.

Common Mistakes Military Folks Make

- Thinking TSP alone will make them rich.

- Sitting in the G fund for 15 years.

- Not investing while renting.

- Panic selling when the market drops

- Not using Roth while income is still low

Avoid those, and you're already ahead.

Where This Fits in the Blueprint

Chapter 1–4 taught you to control the money. Chapter 5 (this one) teaches you to **deploy** the money. The next chapter is where we start building the ladder for scaling. how to go from "I invest" to "I own assets."

Chapter 6

The TSP Advantage: Your Government-Issued Investment Tool

If you wear the uniform or work for the government, you already have access to one of the most powerful wealth-building tools ever created, and most people barely understand it. It's called the Thrift Savings Plan (TSP).

Think of it as the government's version of a 401(k), but with fewer fees, more automation, and guaranteed matching money if you're under the Blended Retirement System. It's not flashy, but it's reliable, and reliability is what wins financial wars. The TSP is not just a retirement account. It's a government-issued wealth engine.

Traditional vs. Roth TSP: Choose Your Weapon

Before you start contributing, you have to choose

how your money goes in: pre-tax or post-tax.

Here's the breakdown in plain language:

Type	How It Works	When You Pay Taxes	Best For
Traditional TSP	Contributions come from your paycheck before taxes.	You pay taxes later, when you withdraw.	If you expect to be in a lower tax bracket in retirement.
Roth TSP	Contributions are made after taxes.	You pay taxes now, but withdraw tax-free later.	If you're early in your career or expect to earn more later.

Example:

Let's say you contribute $500/month.

- With Traditional, you avoid paying tax on that $500 today, but when you retire and take it out, Uncle Sam takes his cut.

- With Roth, you pay tax on the $500 now, but in retirement, it's all yours — every dollar of growth is tax-free.

For most junior to mid-career service members, the Roth option wins because your tax rate is likely lower now than it'll be later when you're earning more.

The 5% Match: Free Money That Too Many Ignore

If you're under the Blended Retirement System (BRS), the government will:

- Automatically contribute 1% of your base pay whether you contribute or not.

- Match up to 4% of your own contributions.

That's a total of 5% extra pay every month and you don't have to do anything except participate. Put simply: if you're not contributing at least 5%, you're throwing away free money.

The Power of Compounding in the TSP

Compounding is the silent weapon of the disciplined. It's when your money earns returns, and those returns start earning returns. Let's say you contribute $500/month from age 25 to 45, earning an average of 7% per year. That equals $120,000 in contributions. But with compounding, it grows to about $260,000.

If you keep it going to age 60, you'll have over $575,000 and that's without ever increasing your contribution. You didn't win the lottery. You just showed up consistently.

Understanding TSP Funds (Simplified)

The TSP gives you six main fund options, each with a different level of risk and reward.

Fund	What It Invests In	Risk	Purpose
G Fund	U.S. government securities	Very Low	Stability, preserves capital
F Fund	Bonds (fixed income)	Low	Slightly better returns than G
C Fund	S&P 500 companies	Moderate	Core U.S. stock market
S Fund	Small & mid-cap U.S. stocks	Higher	Growth and diversification
I Fund	International stocks	Higher	Global exposure
L Funds	Mixture of all above	Varies by target date	Auto-adjusts risk over time

---

Pro Tip:

If you don't want to manage it yourself, pick a Lifecycle (L) Fund that matches your retirement year; it automatically shifts your balance from aggressive to conservative as you age.

Sample TSP Allocations by Age and Rank

You don't need to be perfect; you need to be intentional. Here are practical examples based on age and stage:

Junior Enlisted / Early Career (18–29):
- 10% G Fund
- 10% F Fund
- 40% C Fund
- 25% S Fund
- 15% I Fund

Goal: Aggressive growth with a long runway to ride out market swings.

Mid-Career NCO/Officer (30–40):
- 15% G Fund
- 15% F Fund
- 35% C Fund
- 20% S Fund
- 15% I Fund

Goal: Balance between stability and growth. You've built a base; now protect it while expanding.

Senior / Approaching Retirement (40+):

- 30% G Fund
- 25% F Fund
- 25% C Fund
- 10% S Fund
- 10% I Fund

Goal: Preserve capital and reduce volatility; focus on income stability.

Golden Nugget Tip: Don't Time the Market; Stay in Formation

- The most common mistake service members make with TSP? Jumping in and out based on fear or headlines. Market dips are like training rucks; they're uncomfortable but necessary. When prices drop, your same contribution buys *more shares*. That's called dollar-cost averaging, and it's how long-term investors quietly win. You can't control the market. You can control consistency.

Your TSP Checklist

- Contribute at least 5% for the full government match.
- Choose Roth if you're early in your career or expect to earn more later.

- Set your allocation (or pick an L Fund).

- Don't panic-move when the market dips.

- Increase your contribution 1–2% every promotion.

This isn't a set-and-forget account, it's a slow-burn engine for financial freedom.

From Government Benefit to Personal Leverage

Your TSP is more than a retirement plan, it is a readiness plan. It's the first step toward never depending on a paycheck again. The same government that funds your mission funds your future. You just have to activate it.

Chapter 7

Systems Thinking: How the Wealthy Automate Everything

Discipline will get you started. Systems will keep you winning. Wealthy people don't rely on motivation; they rely on automation. They build systems that make success automatic, even when they're distracted, deployed, or disconnected. That's the difference between *working for your money* and *letting your money work for you.*

Why Systems Thinking Matters

If you're in the military, you already understand systems. There's a process for everything: supply, maintenance, and readiness. No one gets promoted for working harder; they get promoted for building better systems. Money works the same way.

If you're constantly chasing bills, juggling pay-ments, and trying to "remember" to invest, you don't have a money problem; you have a systems problem. Systems thinking turns chaos into control. You create a structure once, and it runs itself.

The 4 Pillars of Financial Automation

Let's break down the core systems that wealthy people use, all of which you can duplicate easily.

1. Automated Income Flow

Your paycheck hits → money moves automati-cally. Create an automatic distribution plan:

- Checking Account (Operations): For bills and spending.

- Savings Account (Reserve): Automatic 10% de-posit each LES.

- Investment Account: Automatic transfer to Roth IRA or brokerage.

- Freedom Fund: Optional account for travel, hobbies, or morale.

Set this up through myPay or your bank. Once it's

done, your entire financial formation runs on autopilot. You never have to "decide" to save again. It just happens.

2. Automated Bill Management

Every month, the same bills hit. The wealthy don't waste brainpower tracking them; they automate them.

Set recurring payments for:

- Rent/Mortgage
- Insurance
- Utilities
- Credit cards (set to pay in full)
- Subscriptions

Then, set one "Money Review Day" per month to check everything. Not daily. Not weekly. Once a month, you review the system, not run it. That's how you stay in command without being buried in admin.

3. Automated Investing

If you have to log in and click "buy," you'll forget. Every good investor has automatic transfers set up:

- **TSP contributions** directly from LES.

- **Roth IRA contributions** set monthly.

- **Brokerage auto-buys** for index funds or ETFs.

Automation removes emotion. When the market dips, your system keeps buying, meaning you're getting investments "on sale" while everyone else panics. This is how you win over decades, not weeks.

4. Automated Tracking & Optimization

Once everything runs itself, you need visibility, not control, but awareness. Wealthy people use **dashboards**, not checklists. They don't ask, "Where did my money go?" They can see it instantly.

Recommended Tools:

- **YNAB (You Need A Budget):** Best for active money management.

- **Empower (formerly Personal Capital):** Free dashboard for net worth and investments.

- **Mint:** Great for beginners and expense tracking.

- **Tiller/Notion:** For spreadsheet lovers who want custom control.

Every 90 days, review:

- Net worth (assets – liabilities)
- Debt-to-income ratio
- Savings rate
- Investment performance

Adjust once per quarter, then let the system run.

Golden Nugget Tip: The Deployment Test

- Ask yourself this: "If I deployed tomorrow for six months, would my money keep moving the same way?" If the answer is no, you need to automate more. That's how the wealthy operate. Their money moves without them. Systems keep your finances mission-ready even when you're not around to supervise.

Workflow Example: The Financial Ops Chain

Here's what a fully automated system might look like:

1. LES hits (1st & 15th)
2. 60% goes to checking → covers bills and living

expenses.

3. 20% goes to savings automatically.

4. 10% goes to investments.

5. 10% goes to "Freedom Fund."

6. Auto-pay handles bills.

7. Monthly dashboard auto-updates your pro-gress.

That's it. No stress, no spreadsheets, no surprises. Your job is not to micromanage; it's to lead the system.

Why Automation Is Freedom

When you automate, you eliminate friction. When you eliminate friction, you eliminate excuses. You'll never feel "too tired" to save again. You'll never forget to invest. The system takes care of the mission. Wealth isn't built by people who have time. It's built by people who build systems.

Chapter 8

Reinvesting the Return: The Growth Cycle

You've fought the debt war. You've built your budget formation. You've automated your money like a system that never sleeps. Now you're earning profit cash flow, dividends, or equity growth. So the question becomes, what *do you do with it?* This is where average earners stop. They save for comfort. Builders keep going. They reinvest for momentum.

The Power of the Growth Cycle

Think of your money like a platoon. When it comes back from the field with experience, you don't discharge it; you retrain it and redeploy it. That's the growth cycle:

Earn → Reinvest → Scale → Earn More → Reinvest Again.

Every dollar has a mission. When you redeploy

profits instead of spending them, you multiply the output of your system.

1. Upgrade Assets, Don't Upgrade Lifestyles

The moment you start winning financially, lifestyle creep tries to sneak in. That's when people buy new cars, eat out more, or upgrade their house just because they can. That's not growth; that's drift. Real growth happens when you take your *surplus* and use it to buy assets that produce *more surplus*.

Example:

- Your rental brings in $400/month net cash flow.

- Instead of spending it, you save it until you can purchase another rental.

- That next property doubles your cash flow.

Now your lifestyle *can* expand later because your income base did first.

2. The Three R's of Reinvestment

Every reinvestment decision falls into one of these three categories:

1. **Reinvest in Assets**—Real estate, index funds, or other income-producing tools.

2. **Reinvest in Skills**—Certifications, courses, or licenses that increase your earning power.

3. **Reinvest in Systems**—Tools or automation that save you time or enhance efficiency.

If an expense doesn't fall under one of those three, it's probably consumption, not growth.

3. Compounding: The Silent Force

Compounding is what separates the disciplined from the average. Let's say you start with $10,000 and earn 10% annually. After one year: $11,000. Leave it alone another year: $12,100. Ten years later: almost $26,000.

But if you add $200 per month, it becomes nearly $50,000. Compounding isn't magic; it's math powered by consistency. The earlier and longer you reinvest, the faster your system multiplies.

4. Scaling Through Reinvestment Strategies

Different stages require different moves. Here's how to think about scaling as your base grows.

Stage	Monthly Surplus	Reinvestment Focus
Starter	$100–$500	Pay debt, build emergency fund, start TSP or IRA
Builder	$500–$1,500	Add index funds, explore small rental or REITs
Scaler	$1,500+	Expand property portfolio, diversify into business ownership
Commander	$5,000+	Delegate management, invest in leadership-level ventures

Your rank in wealth isn't your paycheck; it's your system's rank.

5. Reinvesting Equity: The Hidden Fuel

Homeowners often sit on equity like it's a trophy instead of a tool. That's locked potential. You can tap it strategically to accelerate growth.

Options include:

- **HELOC (Home Equity Line of Credit):** borrow only what you need; ideal for down payments or renovations.

- **Cash-out refinance:** replace your old mortgage with a larger one, taking the difference in cash.

- **Bridge loan:** temporary funding that lets you

buy before you sell.

Used wisely, equity is your silent investor. Just remember leverage should shorten your time to freedom, not extend your debt.

6. The Reinvestment Rhythm

To keep momentum steady:

1. **Set a Review Cycle:** quarterly check of net worth, savings rate, and ROI.

2. **Reallocate:** move profits from low-performing accounts to higher-yield options.

3. **Reserve:** always keep 3–6 months of expenses liquid before reinvesting further.

Every review is like a promotion board for your dollars: keep what performs, and retrain or reassign what doesn't.

Golden Nugget Tip: Separate Progress from Pleasure

- Reward yourself, but separate *reward money* from *growth money*. For example, use 10% of your profit for fun and 90% for reinvestment. That keeps your motivation alive without derailing your mission.

Mission Summary

- Reinvest profits before you increase lifestyle.
- Use the Three R's—Assets, Skills, and Systems as your compass.
- Let compounding and consistency do the heavy lifting.
- Review and redeploy every quarter.

Chapter 9

The Credit Game – How to Build, Protect, and Leverage It

Credit is your quietest rank. You can't wear it on your sleeve, but it determines how much opportunity salutes when you walk in the room. Most people treat credit like a score. Builders treat it like a weapon.

1. What Credit Really Measures

Credit isn't just about borrowing it's about trust. It's the financial equivalent of your reputation in the field.

Lenders use it to gauge:

- **Reliability:** Do you pay on time?

- **Consistency:** How long have you managed credit?

- **Capacity:** How much of your available credit

do you use?

- **Diversity:** Can you handle different types of accounts responsibly?

The goal isn't just to "have credit." It is to *use credit like an asset.*

2. The Five Ranks of Your Credit Score

Category	Weight	What It Means
Payment History	35%	Never miss a payment—ever. One late payment can drop your score by 100 points.
Credit Utilization	30%	Keep balances under 30% of available credit (ideally under 10%).
Length of Credit History	15%	Older accounts show stability. Keep your oldest card open.
New Credit Inquiries	10%	Too many applications look desperate. Space them out.
Credit Mix	10%	Variety helps—credit cards, auto loan, TSP loan, or mortgage all signal balance.

Each one ranks you on discipline, not income. A junior enlisted member can outrank a colonel in credit if they play smarter.

3. Building Credit from the Ground Up

If you're starting fresh (or recovering):

1. **Get a secured credit card** – backed by your own deposit.

2. **Use it for one small recurring bill** and pay in full every month.

3. **Add rent reporting services** to credit bureaus if you rent.

4. **Set auto payments** for minimums to avoid accidental lates.

5. **Track your score monthly** through Experian or Credit Karma.

Small, consistent moves create big long-term trust.

4. Protecting Your Credit Rank

Financial attacks don't always come from hackers they come from complacency.

Here's your defense plan:

- **Freeze your credit** when not actively applying. It stops identity theft.

- **Use alerts** for transactions and new accounts.

- **Dispute errors** immediately with bureaus (you can do this online for free).

- **Avoid cosigning** unless you're ready to pay the whole loan yourself.

A clean credit profile is your armor. Keep it intact.

5. Leverage: Using Credit to Build Wealth

When you understand leverage, credit turns from a liability into a ladder.

Examples:

- **VA Loan:** 0% down payment but 100% ownership opportunity.

- **Business credit cards:** fund marketing or startup costs interest-free for 12 months.

- **HELOC:** tap home equity to invest in income-producing assets.

The key rule → borrow to *buy cash flow,* not to buy comfort.

6. Credit Utilization Tactics

- **Raise your limits** without raising your spending.

- **Pay balances twice a month.** That keeps your utilization low on reporting dates.

- **Keep your old accounts open** to extend history.

- **Ask for interest reductions** after 6 months of on-time payments.

These micro-habits quietly add 50–100 points over time.

7. When to Use Credit for Advantage

Smart use cases:

- Buying real estate that produces rent.

- Consolidating high-interest debt into a lower-rate loan.

- Starting a business with a clear plan for ROI.

Bad use cases:

- Cars you can't afford.

- Furniture you don't need.

- Vacations on a balance.

If the loan doesn't generate income or improve your capacity to earn it's not leverage; it's weight.

8. Credit as a Team Game

For dual-income families or spouses:

- Maintain individual credit lines and joint accounts.

- Rotate who takes primary roles on big purchases to build both profiles.

- Teach teenagers about credit early by making them authorized users on low-limit cards.

Credit discipline is a household skill not just a personal one.

The "Five for Freedom" Rule

Keep these five accounts active for a balanced score:

1. Two credit cards.

2. One auto loan (or installment loan).

3. One mortgage.

4. One personal line of credit or secured card.

Five active, managed lines show the credit bureaus you can handle complexity.

Mission Summary

- Treat credit like a rank you earn through discipline.

- Build slow, steady, and on-purpose.

- Protect it like your security clearance.
- Use leverage only to create cash flow, not consume it.

Chapter 10

Family Finance Ops: Building Together

Money shouldn't be a solo mission. In the military, every operation succeeds because everyone knows the plan, their role, and the mission objective. Your household finances should work the same way. When only one person understands the money, the family's future depends on that one person's presence. When everyone understands, the mission continues no matter what.

1. The Family Financial Formation

Think of your family as a unit. Each person plays a role, even if not everyone brings income.

Role	Focus Area	Example
Commander (You)	Leadership, vision, and decisions	Sets goals and priorities
XO (Spouse/ Partner)	Operations and accountability	Manages bill payments and tracking
Future Leaders (Kids)	Learning through exposure	Understand saving, earning, and value

A family's wealth plan only works when everyone is trained for their lane.

2. The Briefing: Communication is Currency

Arguments about money rarely come from lack of money, they come from lack of clarity.

Here's how to fix that:

- **Hold a monthly "Money Brief."**

  15–30 minutes max. Review what came in, what went out, and what's next.

- **Use visual dashboards.**

  Apps like Monarch Money, YNAB, or even a shared Google Sheet keep everyone synced.

- **Lead with goals, not guilt.**

The goal isn't to assign blame; it's to align focus.

Money talks work best when everyone feels ownership, not pressure.

3. Teaching Kids the Mission Early

You don't have to wait for your kids to turn 18 to start building financial literacy. Every allowance, every birthday gift, every trip to the store is a teachable moment.

Simple systems:

- **The 3-Envelope Rule:** Give, Save, Spend.

- **Junior Investor Accounts:** Custodial brokerage accounts let kids watch compounding happen.

- **Model the behavior:** Kids copy what they see, not what they hear.

If your child can name TikTok stars, they can learn to name their investment account too.

4. The Spousal Advantage

In dual-income or dual-military households, the

power is in coordination. Separate finances often create overlap or missed opportunities.

To maximize efficiency:

- Combine savings goals but keep individual spending accounts for freedom.

- Align TSP contributions and insurance decisions.

- Sync PCS planning to maximize VA loan use and equity rotation.

Two paychecks should equal two engines, not two different flight paths.

5. The "Family CFO" Concept

Every household needs a designated CFO the one who keeps systems running. This isn't about control; it's about clarity.

Duties include:

- Tracking net worth.

- Overseeing automation setup.

- Managing communication with tax, insurance, and investment partners.

Switch who holds the title annually; it builds shared skill and accountability.

6. Building Generational Conversations

At some point, your financial mission has to move from secrecy to strategy. Talk about wills, insurance, and legacy openly especially with aging parents or young adult children. Avoiding the subject doesn't protect feelings; it endangers futures. Transparency builds trust and preparedness.

7. Family Meetings that Move the Needle

Here's a sample monthly rhythm:

Week	Focus	Action
Week 1	Review Income & Bills	Check auto-drafts, make adjustments
Week 2	Growth Review	Update net worth tracker
Week 3	Education	Watch a financial video or read a short article as a family
Week 4	Reward	Celebrate hitting savings or debt goals

Consistency beats intensity. It's not about perfect meetings, it's about persistent awareness.

Golden Nugget Tip: Talk About Money Like You Talk About the Mission

- The military doesn't whisper about strategy, and families shouldn't whisper about finances. Replace shame with structure. When everyone's informed, everyone's empowered.

Mission Summary

- Run your household like a team, not a solo act.

- Hold monthly briefings and keep communication clear.

- Teach kids early — exposure equals empowerment.

- Rotate responsibility to build mutual financial strength.

- Talk about legacy and long-term plans openly.

Chapter 11

The Portfolio Mindset – From Earner to Owner

Most people spend their entire careers mastering one skill earning. They clock in, trade time for money, and repeat. But the real shift happens when you stop seeing yourself as a worker *in* the system and start operating as an owner *of* systems. The wealthy don't just earn, they allocate.

1. The Owner's Mindset

Being an owner isn't about having millions. It's about understanding leverage, delegation, and duplication.

- An earner asks: *How much can I make this month?*

- An owner asks: *How much can I make without being there?*

That single question separates those who *work for money* from those whose *money works for them*.

2. Turning Income Streams into Assets

Think of your finances like a base with multiple supply lines. If one gets cut off, others keep you mission-ready. Every stream of income should do one of three things:

1. Produce cash flow now.

2. Grow equity over time.

3. Increase future earning power.

Stream	Type	Example
Active	Immediate cash flow	Your primary job, side hustle
Semi-Passive	Cash with light management	Rental property, small business
Passive	Self-sustaining income	Index fund dividends, royalties

The key is to convert active income into passive ownership.

3. From Soldier to CEO: Thinking in Systems

You already understand systems; it's how the military runs. Operations, logistics, maintenance, and finance, each with structure and accountability. Apply the same to your money:

- **Operations:** automate bills and investments.

- **Logistics:** make sure every dollar knows its mission.

- **Maintenance:** review and adjust quarterly.

- **Finance:** measure ROI on time, money, and energy.

Every dollar should have a duty description and a measurable result.

4. Your First Portfolio Map

Your portfolio isn't just investments, it's your full financial ecosystem. Here's a sample "Blueprint Stack" for structure:

Tier	Asset Type	Purpose
Tier 1	Emergency Fund	Security and flexibility
Tier 2	TSP / IRA	Long-term growth
Tier 3	Real Estate	Appreciation + cash flow
Tier 4	Index Funds / ETFs	Steady, scalable growth
Tier 5	Business or Brand	Freedom + legacy creation

When you can see every tier, you can start balancing them just like mission priorities.

5. Scaling through Delegation

Eventually, ownership requires trust. Hire a CPA, use a property manager, partner with a financial planner. You're not giving up control you're buying back time. And time is the most profitable currency on the planet.

6. Track Your Net Worth, Not Your Paycheck

Income pays bills. Net worth builds freedom. Start tracking your asset-minus-debt balance quarterly. Watch how it moves. That's your financial fitness score. Over time, you'll notice something powerful: you stop caring how much you make in a month and start caring how much you keep and grow.

7. The Ownership Progression

1. Earn actively.

2. Automate savings and investing.

3. Buy assets that create income.

4. Use profits to buy more assets.

5. Delegate management.

6. Focus on strategy and freedom.

That's the path from worker → investor → architect → owner.

Golden Nugget Tip: Think of Money Like Machinery

- If your systems require you to push every button manually, you don't own machinery, you *are* the machinery. Build systems that run when you're asleep, deployed, or retired. That's ownership.

Mission Summary

- The goal isn't a raise, it's replacement income.

- Build multiple income supply lines.

- Track net worth, not just paychecks.

- Delegate to scale your time and impact.

- Always ask: *Is this a job or an asset?*

Chapter 12

Golden Nuggets – The Blueprint Recap

Every mission ends with an after-action review. This is yours. These aren't new lessons, they're the distilled wisdom from every chapter in this book. Read them fast. Memorize what hits. Then act on one today.

Mindset

- You don't need to make more money, you need to manage what you already have better.

- Freedom doesn't come from income; it comes from *structure*.

- Your paycheck is your first investor treat it like one.

- If you can follow orders, you can follow a budget.

Budgeting

- Every dollar needs a mission.

- Automate bills and savings so your discipline isn't tested daily.

- Track your money weekly, not monthly. Waiting 30 days is how missions fail.

- Eliminate "ghost expenses" subscriptions, impulse buys, and food delivery that eat your raise.

Debt Discipline

- Debt isn't evil; disorganized debt is.

- Consolidate, automate, and attack high interest first.

- Don't just pay off debt, replace it with assets that pay *you*.

- The goal isn't zero debt. The goal is *controlled leverage*.

Investing

- Start early. Time beats timing.

- Never invest in something you don't understand.

- Automate contributions so you never "forget to invest."

- Index funds are like the infantry, steady, reliable, effective.

Credit

- Credit is your silent clearance level. Guard it.

- 750 isn't a number, it's access.

- Borrow to build, not to buy comfort.

- A credit card paid in full monthly is a financial power-up, not a liability.

TSP & Retirement

- Treat your TSP like rent non-negotiable.

- Matching contributions are *free money*. Leaving them unused is like ignoring hazard pay.

- Adjust allocations as your mission changes, growth early, stability later.

Systems

- Automate everything you can: bills, investing, savings.

- What gets automated gets done.

- Your system should work even if you're deployed, busy, or between duty stations.

- Review quarterly, not annually the wealthy iterate faster.

Reinvestment

- Every extra dollar should have a future job.

- Don't upgrade lifestyle, upgrade leverage.

- Compound your wins: use profit to buy more profit.

- Reinvestment turns momentum into mastery.

Credit & Ownership

- Own assets that appreciate.

- Use good credit to acquire, not to consume.

- Protect your credit like your DD-214, one error can haunt you for years.

- The goal: when you borrow, it's to buy something that pays you back.

Family Finance Ops

- Wealth is a team sport.

- Brief monthly, celebrate progress, and communicate constantly.

- Teach your kids now not when they move out.

- Financial literacy is the inheritance that never depreciates.

Portfolio Mindset

- Track net worth like your fitness score.

- Replace hours with assets.

- Every paycheck: earn → invest → reinvest → repeat.

- Ownership is the final promotion.

Golden Nugget Recap Mantra

→ Discipline creates freedom.

→ Systems sustain discipline.

→ Ownership creates options.

Live by those three, and you'll always outrank your money.

Chapter 13

Conclusion – Discipline Creates Freedom

You've made it to the end, but this isn't the end. It's the transfer of command.

From theory → execution.

From paycheck → portfolio.

From follower → owner.

1. The Real Definition of Freedom

Freedom isn't just about rank, money, or location. It's about options. The freedom to choose where you live, how you spend your time, and who you spend it with. Money doesn't buy happiness, it buys space to create it.

Every lesson in this book is designed to give you that space: structure, confidence, and control over the one thing most people ignore until it controls them.

2. The Power of Discipline

When you were in uniform, discipline was survival. In wealth-building, discipline is freedom. You don't need to be a financial expert you just need consistency.

Automate → Track → Reinvest.

Do it long enough, and the results become inevitable. Discipline turns your paycheck into a soldier that never sleeps. Every dollar you deploy carries out a mission: protect, provide, and multiply.

3. Your Blueprint in Action

Here's your simplified playbook:

1. **Audit the Mission** – List your income, expenses, and assets.

2. **Eliminate Weak Links** – Attack high-interest debt.

3. **Automate the System** – Bills, savings, and investing on autopilot.

4. **Invest Like a Commander** – Prioritize growth over gratification.

5. **Reinvest the Return** – Turn profit into momentum.

6. **Build the Team** – Involve your spouse, kids, and future.

Repeat that cycle until your money is running missions without you.

4. The Final Mindset Shift

When you realize money is just a tool of discipline, everything changes. It's not about getting rich, it's about becoming reliable. Reliable for your family, your future, and your freedom. You've already proven you can follow a system the military taught you that. Now it's time to follow your own.

5. Your Call to Action

You've got the tools. You've got the mindset. Now build the life that doesn't depend on payday. *"Freedom isn't found at retirement, it's built paycheck by paycheck."*

— Ask Antwaun

Epilogue

The Mission Never Ends

When I first joined the Army, I thought freedom came from the uniform from serving, ranking up, and doing my part. But what I've learned since leaving is that *true freedom* doesn't come from a paycheck, promotion, or deployment. It comes from control. over your time, your money, and your future.

For years, I believed discipline was something the Army gave me. But discipline was always mine to command I just hadn't learned how to apply it outside the formation. Once I did, everything changed. My finances got structure. My goals became missions. And every dollar I earned started working harder than I did.

This book isn't just about budgeting or investing it's about taking back command of your life. The systems you've learned here are the same ones I built from scratch after I hung up the uniform. They're not theory they're field-tested. And if they worked for me, they'll work for you.

You've now got the blueprint. The next step is execution. Whether you're active duty, a veteran, or a military family member, your financial mission doesn't end here it begins now. Every PCS, every paycheck, every decision is a new opportunity to build something that lasts beyond your service. So keep the momentum. Keep learning. Keep building. And when you're ready to turn your blueprint into a fully operational plan let's make it personal.

About The Author

Antwaun Hill is a U.S. Army veteran, real estate professional, and educator based in Hawaii. After 13 years of active-duty service, he transitioned to civilian life and discovered how misunderstood military financial benefits truly were, including his own.

That realization sparked a mission: to help service members, veterans, and military families use the VA loan, BAH, and PCS opportunities to build lasting wealth. As the founder of **Ask Antwaun**, he's become a trusted voice for military real estate education, blending strategy, storytelling, and empowerment.

Through his brand and book series, *BAH Means Buy A House*, Antwaun continues to teach one core message: "You already have the benefits. You just need to learn how to use them."

Follow him on Instagram **@AskAntwaun**

Contact: **AskAntwaun@gmail.com**

Other books in this series